A Life Worth Living, Again

Leovita Cabrera

BookLeaf Publishing

Presentation by *BookLeaf Publishing*

Web: www.bookleafpub.com

E-mail: info@bookleafpub.com

ISBN: 9789357615945

First edition 2022

Dedicated to my parents and my siblings (Zeida, Zoel, Zannella, and Lenore) because in what's left of our lives, I still seek ways to make you all proud... I'd also like to dedicate this to myself, a toast if I may say so, to finally letting go of trying to be who I once was and learning to love and embrace who I am now.

ACKNOWLEDGEMENT

The creation of this book would not have been possible without my biggest motivators: Le'Andre Jerah Cabrera and Daniel Diesel C. Quitugua. Because of you two, my desire to be better than I was yesterday burns greater than ever. The inspiration behind this book goes to one of my closest friends and fellow author, Cecile Katricia PN. Lastly, to my cousin, Brittney DLC Y., I would not have joined this challenge without the unconditional love and support you continue to smother me with. Ew, David.

My First Love

His eyes told a story of our love
His arms felt like Home
His voice comforted me
Whenever I felt alone

Soon after, his eyes strayed
His arms sheltered someone else
His voice became her comfort
And he left me by myself

My first love; my first heartbreak

Play Or Be Played

Bus-stop make-out sessions
Our names on rice in a necklace
His love was refreshing
His love caused me no stress

My oldest sister really liked him
But he wanted so much of my time
And giving it to him
Made me feel like my life wasn't mine

Too scared to lose myself to love again
I took my love back in the worst of ways
I hurt him before he could hurt me
With love, it was either play or be played

Because I Loved Her

My pain was for more than one reason
My pain was because of more than one person
I was hurting and I wanted help
I wanted help because I was hurting

I cried for help through my self-inflicted cuts
I screamed inside as my blood flowed out
My tears fell, my body went numb,
And one night, I figured it out

Without the lies and false hope
An addict's love and my cuts hurt the same
There's an "escape" in going numb
And power in that I caused my own pain

I craved to feel nothing
While still wanting to be heard
I left evidence of broken razors
And more than one blood-stained shirt

A very close friend of mine
"Shorty" asked me to stop
But I was too dependent on it for relief
So, I told her I could not

Not long after, she stopped breathing.
And I stopped because I loved her.

Out Of The Closet

Is Therese your girlfriend?
No.

Is R***** your girlfriend?
Yeah.

My Mom pulled me out of the closet that day
My oldest sister and my Dad weren't supportive
at the time
But whether whoever liked it or not
I promised myself I would never hide

Five Years Too Long

This was originally supposed to be about the
relationship we had
But all I want to say about that

-is-

I waited five years too long
To realize it was time and effort wasted
I was young and you were dumb
And I'm glad we didn't make it

As always though, I wish you the best
May your marriage with your side piece
continue to prevail

Never Say Never

He abused his girlfriend
And I couldn't understand
Why she allowed him to do that to her
Why she defended that man

I told her I could never-

He pushed me so hard
I was down on the floor
He ran from the scene
As I hurt deep within my core

This man put his hands on me
In ways I said I'd never allow
The very next day, I was missing him
And we ended up back together somehow

I ate my words like I was starving
But I carved and carried my cross
This man was my abuser
But to me, this man was LOVE

My parents tried to keep us apart
But I always found my way back to him
The abuse became more normal

And the light inside me started to dim

Our bad days were horrible
Our good days were better
Our relationship taught me
To Never Say Never

I finally decided to leave him
And leave him I did
Or so I thought because I found out
I was pregnant with his kid

Baby Blues

I left your Dad so they could work things out
I left your Dad because he was hurting me
I left your Dad because I deserved better
But I never left him because I took you with me

When that test came out positive
I was both happy and scared
But I became selfish with your Dad
I wanted him to show he cared

I wanted us to be a family
Even after the abuse
I wanted him to be closer to us
I was having baby blues

One day, he denied you were his
Another day, you were his and his alone
Long-distance was hard to maintain
When he wasn't picking up his phone

It was an emotional rollercoaster
And I wanted to get off
I couldn't force your Dad to choose me
I finally had enough

I remember caressing my belly that night
Talking to you in the dark
Apologizing for always feeling so sad
For exposing you to my breaking heart

Left Before You Came

My Dad eased my worries
When I called my parents because I was spotting
He told me that my Mom bled too
And that it was probably nothing

I tried my best to be happy
I tried my best to stay calm
I tried my best to be okay
With being single and being your Mom

The night I vowed to be better for you
I fell asleep in peace
What I woke up to was a nightmare
A horror movie scene

It was past midnight
Blood soaked through my jeans
I rushed to the bathroom thinking
"I hope this isn't-please don't let this be-"

Scared to think or say it out loud
I showered and hoped I was wrong
But as I washed the blood off me
I realized the worst was yet to come

A lot of -I don't know what's- came out of me
My feet were surrounded by it all
My sister came in and I spoke those dreaded
words
"I think I had a miscarriage, but I don't know"

Before I left, I picked up what I thought was you
And placed you in your Dad's shirt
The doctor told me to push and said you might
have come out
But the ultrasound was to be sure

There was absolutely no trace of you
I was drowning in grief and pain
I couldn't fully process what was going on
I just knew you left before you came

Everything Happens For A Reason

I was depressed after losing you
I could barely get out of bed
Didn't have an appetite for food or life
Sometimes, I woke up and wished I was dead

They said everything happens for a reason
They said it just wasn't meant to be
They said God needed you for something greater
Than a life here on Earth with me

None of it made sense
None of it sounded right
Losing you was the hardest thing
I ever had to go through in my life

Was I too late at promising better for you?
Did I deserve to feel more pain?
If God took you from me, was he at fault?
Or was I the one to blame?

My biggest purpose was to take care of you
And I couldn't even keep you safe inside me
It felt pointless to keep living my life
As a Mother without her Baby

Too Good To Be True

I first met him at the airport
We talked before he walked up to his gate
He had dreads, he was cute,
And the conversation was great

I didn't express my attraction to him
Because I already had someone I loved
But that didn't last and the next time I saw him
He immediately recognized who I was

We were at GIG and I passed by him
As I was walking inside
He looked at me with excited eyes
And I realized who he was that night

He expressed his interest in me
But my life was a mess
I could tell he wanted to save me
Like a damsel in distress

The year we reunited
Was the year I was addicted to escaping
Weed, alcohol, my two full-time jobs
I didn't want him to save me

I didn't want to be his girlfriend
I only wanted to be his friend
Because my friendships are forever
And my relationships always end

I couldn't risk falling in love
And having my heart shattered
I couldn't risk him switching up on me
As if I never mattered

He understood where I was coming from
He was patient as ever
But let me tell you about this man
Who deserved so much better

He bought my Mom flowers for Mother's Day
He brought food to me at my night job
He spent time with me whenever he could
He always asked how I was

He went off-island for a competition
But he had so much planned while he was gone
He had food dropped off at my day job every
day
He had his friends serenade me with a song

When he got back, he surprised me with gifts
When he brought me home late at night, he
always walked me to my door

He was perfect in every way
Everything I could have hoped for in a man and
more

The thing is, I didn't want a man at that time
My heart was too broken and bruised
Compared to him, I was so damaged
And he seemed too good to be true

I was never enough for my exes
What chance did I have with this guy?
I didn't deem myself worthy
Of being a part of his life

So, I pushed him away
To find someone more deserving
Someone who could give him more
Than I could have ever given

Team 7 AM

My first group of friends
That became family
A year of nonstop joy and laughter
Burning and drinking

SOJA, Mtn Dew and Smirnoff
Monster and Skyy Vodka, dancing all night
Chili-blocking the tourists
Involuntary being part of a fight

03-29-13: Thank you for lighting candles
And releasing balloons
That was a very special day for me
And I'm glad to have spent it with all of you

Team 7 AM, miss and love you.

Rainbow Baby

I ignored him for a year
And I thought I moved on
But the minute I received an e-mail from him
I realized I was wrong

I thought I blocked him from everything
And I knew he moved to the states
He gave me his number, so I called him
His voice still made my heart race

The butterflies in my stomach resurfaced
Once buried under layers of pain
My caramel cheeks turned rosy red
And I was in love with him again

A year apart from each other meant a clean slate
But it was as if we never even parted ways
It was as if he never hurt me
And we only had good days

I wanted to be closer to him
So, I decided to move
Team 7AM grew smaller
And it became easier to choose

Choose me over the stress
I was facing at home
Being with him sounded better
Than being stressed alone

Plus, the idea of having one baby daddy meant a
lot to me
A chance to create another life together
We had an Angel Baby
A Rainbow Baby would've made things better

Sunshine

Not much changed
From how we used to be back home
The abuse there was a little worse
But out here, I was really on my own

Back home, you threw change at me
Burned me with a cigarette on my back
Slapped, kicked, punched, and shoved me
Hurled me across 13 Fisherman

This time was worse than the first time
Both times involved the use of drugs
But if I could love an addict
I could accept an abusive addict's love

My brother hoped I would choose myself over
you
And at first, I did
But after you left for Connecticut
I couldn't do it

The misery of being with you
Was more desirable than not
You eventually flew back out to me
And I once again chose our love

We took a few buses out to nowhere
With nothing to our name
And excluding the abuse
Things were beginning to change

We both had steady jobs
Shared a car and a place
I was finally seeing some sunshine
After all those months of rainy days

Light Inside Me

The apartment and car were nice
But our bills piled up
With his child support and everything else
I took on a second job

Even with that, it was hard
We were always so stressed
He didn't like how I managed our finances
But I did my very best

I worked all day and night
I made sure our bills were paid
I made sure we had a place to live
I made sure we had food on our plate

He didn't enjoy working for nothing
Didn't like not having money to spend
So, I let him take over our finances
Hoping the nagging would end

I couldn't rest on my days off
He constantly called to make sure I was alone
Surprise visits to my night job
When he wasn't blowing up the phone

If I laughed at a man's joke
I was accused of sleeping with him
Endless accusations, name-calling, and more
Made the light inside me continue to dim

I learned not to make eye contact with people
Only speak when spoken to
Living with and loving the enemy
I trained myself on what not to do

To prevent another war from happening
And spare me from any battles
I tried to be what he wanted me to be
To fit his very mold

Our finances took a turn for the worst
We were drowning in debt
The stress came back, this time heavier
And I remained his definition of perfect

It wasn't enough, he still wanted to hurt me
And I couldn't understand why
So, that was the beginning of
When the light inside me died

His Monster

I called my parents when we fought sometimes
And they'd try to calm things down over the
phone
I hated myself for doing that to them
But I was all on my own

He despised me for exposing that part of him
Because people didn't know
Everyone loved him and enjoyed his company
Because his monster never showed

The monster that woke me up
In the middle of the night
As I was trying to rest before a full day of work
His monster wanted to fight

And when I tried to argue my case
He hit me because I was talking
And when I kept my mouth shut
He hit me because I wasn't talking

Everything I did was wrong
And I started to feel scared
I assumed he was using drugs again
Because all the signs were there

The signs of his abuse though
His monster was smart not to let it show
So, unless I opened up to you
There was no way you would have known

His monster messed up once
Squeezed my face so hard, it bruised
I couldn't go to work until I got makeup
To cover up my black and blues

His monster punched my ribs so hard
It hurt just to breathe
It hurt to laugh, it hurt to talk
It hurt to cough and sneeze

His monster hit my face at Walmart
My glasses fell and broke
His hits were getting harder
And he started to choke

On our way to my work one morning
His monster wanted to play
He talked and I talked back
And I knew it was going to be a long day

His monster argued and I argued back
My glasses broke again as he punched all over
my head

Then he stopped, put his hand inside my pants,
And held tightly onto my pocket

I wanted to fight back
But I calmed myself down
Even though I was terrified
Because he turned the car around

His monster was driving fast
Still holding me by my jeans
I was too scared to take my pants off and run
Because I couldn't really see

His monster took a different way home
Surrounded by trees and nothing else
"This man is about to kill me."
I thought to myself

I thought about how my parents would feel
To find out I was dead so far from home
And that was the day I decided to get away
And that I was better off alone

Jonas Saved Me

My coworker picked me up
Helped me with my bags
Three years in Texas with my ex
And two bags were all I had

I left my ex with everything
Our car, our place, our phone
My coworker took me to his house
And showed me my new home

My whole life changed
I was relieved to get away
But I'll never forget
How Jonas saved me that day

To my Jasper Brookshire Brother's/Tobacco
Barn family,
Thank you for everything.

Cold Turkey

I did what I could
To distract me from my pain
I had weed, alcohol, and companionship
But I still felt like I was going insane

I even found love when I least expected it
But I was leaving in two weeks
Pills made me happier
Smiling and spiraling uncontrollably

I didn't know pills were his weakness
To me, they were okay
They let me think outside my box
And kept me up for days

I was okay with all of that
Because they made me numb
It wasn't until he dozed off and swerved off the
road
That I realized something needed to be done

He bought more pills
But I wanted to slow down
I got in the car with them one night
And we went to someone's house

I don't even remember what happened
I just remember sitting on the side
Pretty sure I lied to the cops
When they asked for my name that night

One day he picked up ten more pills
And we were already on a high
He freaked me out
Taking two pills at a time

He took six pills within a few hours
And he dozed off on the road again
I swallowed the last four pills
Thinking better me than him

We went to his sister's place
Not the highlight of my life
Embarrassed to be there in that state
She saw me at my MOST high

I still wanted to be with him
But I didn't want to be that gone
I told him the minute I flew away from there
No more vices-I was done

I kept my word and cold turkey quit everything.
I wanted him to do the same.

My "If Only"

I was single and hurting
We started talking again
I didn't expect much from her
But the comfort of a friend

I realized there were feelings involved
Her situation made it hard
She was married and had kids
But she claimed I still had her heart

I thought I'd given up on love
But being with her sounded nice
So, I gave in to the idea
Of loving someone else's wife

We communicated daily
Random postcards and letters
Whenever I was feeling down,
She always made me feel better

Tragedy fell on her end
She had to fly back home
She had a few hours in paradise
It was our chance to be alone

I confessed something to her
And she paid it no mind
She just wanted to be with me
To make use of our time

Her kisses rid me of my insecurities
Her warm embrace felt right
She wasn't rightfully mine to love
But she was mine that night

We used to mess around on Saipan
No pressure involved
We both had other halves in our lives
And both of them didn't know

We were content with what we were
We were just friends and that was fine
She kissed me one day and from that day on
We made out all the time

Time passed and we moved on
She left and I got with my ex
She made it back home and reached out to me
But I didn't go see her, out of respect

I knew I had feelings for her at that time
So, it was better to stay away
More time passed and our lives changed
But our feelings stayed the same

We made it work for a little
Our secret love affair
Something happened unexpectedly
And I understood that she was scared

We grew in love then grew apart
After she did something that really hurt me
She wasn't just my "What If"
She was also my "If Only"

Cops And Robbers

They wanted us to meet
Their friends, both single and free
I ended up liking him
And he acted like he liked me

He made me laugh
He kept me warm at night
He surprised me with Valentine's gifts
He gave me his time

He stood me up one night
And I was so confused
Why did he make me feel loved and cared for
Just to make me feel so used?

We went through a little more of life together
Before our communication dissolved to nothing
I was thankful for him and everything
But I wanted more than I was getting

A year or so later
I met another guy
I made him wait a couple of months
Before I decided to give him a try

Sweet promises of little nothings
A hope for happiness once again
I let him be my boyfriend
And he let me be his secret friend

We were only a couple
In his apartment in his room
His two-story apartment
The one past St. Jude

We never went out together
But we sometimes met by chance
One time he got jealous
When another guy asked me to dance

That guy held his hand out
So, I put my hand in his hand
And when I turned around
My boyfriend pulled me to dance

He introduced me to his friends
And I didn't feel like he was hiding me anymore
But he stopped wanting to be with me
And for why, I'm not so sure

I went from dating ex-convicts to dating cops
And they all sucked as lovers
Didn't matter which side of the bars
Some cops were just as bad as the robbers

My Family's Keeper

The youngest of five children
In a middle-class home
I am the only one with
No children of my own

Took it upon myself
To take the role of second provider
I worked to support my family
To make the weight on my Dad's shoulders
lighter

From age sixteen to now
That was the only life I knew
So, when I can't provide for their wants or needs
I feel I'm of no use

Sometimes my load gets heavy
And sometimes I want to cry
Sometimes I wished my older siblings supported
me
Sometimes, I wished they'd at least try

It's hard sometimes being my family's keeper.

Even If I Die

For most of my life, I wanted to find and keep
love.
Now, I just want to find myself and be my very
best.
And now that I'm further along in my journey,
I want to lay my past to rest.

Say goodbye to my insecurities.
Let go of all my flaws.
Love me and be better for me.
Because I am way more than enough.

And even if I die single,
This life I live will be worth it in the end.
Because though life repeatedly tried to knock me
down,
I learned to make my life worth living, again.